PORTRAIT OF
RICHMONDSHIRE

HENRIETTA BYRNE

HALSGROVE

First published in Great Britain in 2010

Copyright © Henrietta Byrne 2010

British Library Cataloguing-in-Publication Data
A CIP record for this title is available from the British Library

ISBN 978 1 84114 915 8

HALSGROVE
Halsgrove House,
Ryelands Industrial Estate,
Bagley Road, Wellington, Somerset TA21 9PZ
Tel: 01823 653777   Fax: 01823 216796
email: sales@halsgrove.com

Part of the Halsgrove group of companies.
Information on all Halsgrove titles is available at: www.halsgrove.com

Printed and bound in India on behalf of JFDi Print Services Ltd

Introduction

When I was telling people about this book, I was surprised to hear them say "Not another book on the Dales"! Their fears were allayed when they understood that it would be a pictorial book on Richmond town and its surrounding area and not the Dales. As one of the Richmond advertising leaflets quotes "Richmond, North Yorkshire is Britain's best kept secret . . ." So why not have a photographic book to support this statement.

The name Richmond originates from Richemont in Normandy. There are over 50 other Richmonds in the world, but the first Richmond was founded in North Yorkshire in 1071 by Alan Rufus. He had the castle built on lands granted to him by William the Conqueror. Richmond Castle was completed in 1086; it consisted of a 100 foot-high keep with walls encompassing the area now known as the Market Place. The keep is the only surviving part of the castle and, given its height, can be seen from all areas of the town. The castle is open to visitors and is maintained by English Heritage. Richmond prospered from the Swaledale wool and lead mining industries throughout the seventeenth and eighteenth centuries. It is from the latter century that the town's Georgian architecture dates, examples of which can be found in the Market Place, Newbiggin and Frenchgate. The Market Place is a large cobbled area with an array of shops, eateries and places to stay.

Although the town and castle have had a peaceful history, it has strong military ties which continue to this day. There is evidence in the castle dungeons that conscientious objectors were imprisoned there during the Great War (this area of the castle is not open to the public). The largest garrison in England is three miles up the road in Catterick. In 1873 Richmond became the hometown to the Green Howard Regiment and their Regimental Museum and Headquarters is housed in Trinity church located in the centre of the Market Place.

Apart from the shops, pubs and tearooms, Richmond has the impressive Georgian Theatre Royal, an eighteenth-century playhouse. The theatre was founded by an actor, Samuel Butler, in 1788. The theatre probably experienced financial problems during the 1800s, when records show low attendances, and it was subsequently closed as a theatre until 1963, when it was restored and reopened. Staying on the theatrical theme Richmond and the Dales are great locations for the TV and film industry – notably for "All Creatures Great & Small" and a "Woman of Substance".

The River Swale passes through Richmond. It rises 2000 feet above sea level in Birkdale, meandering down through Swaledale and eventually joining up with the River Ouse. It is one of the fastest flowing rivers in England and can be seen cascading over the falls in Richmond. The falls are located in the leafy park area known as the Batts. When flooded the falls are a spectacular sight to see and draw many a visitor. However, in 2000 the flood water and velocity of the river caused severe damage and partial collapse of one of the arch supports on Mercury Bridge disabling a main route into the town for a number of months.

The surrounding villages and hamlets are picturesque set against the hilly back drops of the Dales or the agricultural fields in the flatter regions of the shire. Throughout there are wonderful landscapes which are particularly inspiring.

I am privileged to live in Richmond and hope that this book acts as a happy memory of your visit to this delightful market town and surrounding area. As they say today, enjoy!

Richmond Castle keep –
100 feet tall, towering
above the town.

The castle keep can be viewed
from all corners of the town:
here it is seen from Frenchgate.

Viewing the castle from above – the industrial estate provides a good viewpoint especially on a summer's evening.

Viewing the castle from below – the Green provides a striking view of the castle.

Above:
The castle viewed from Culloden Tower, a folly on
the opposite hill looking directly towards it.

Right:
Panoramic view showing the castle in its entirety from Sleegill.

One of the castle gates –
this is between the Barr
and Cornforth Hill.

Cornforth Hill terraces bathing in late summer sunshine.

New Road leads down from the Market Place and Newbiggin to the Green.

The Green is a popular place to live as it is near to the river and woodland walks.

An autumnal
view of the Green.

An assortment of houses facing the Green – note all the pot plants decorating the front of each house.

A close-up of a house front on the Green – the residents are keen on their gardening!

Two views of Culloden Tower –
it used to stand derelict but it
has now been converted into a
delightful holiday cottage.
It stands on a hill overlooking
the castle.

Culloden Tower in winter.

Looking down on the roofs from Lombard's Wynd on a cold and snowy morning.

Winter sunrise —
top of Frenchgate.

The War Memorial stands proudly at the top of Frenchgate. Remembrance Sunday sees the laying down of poppy wreaths.

Left::
Poppy field in front of
Oliver Duckett's Tower.

Right:
A recent poppy wreath.

Frenchgate is one of the cobbled streets leading into the town.

Middle Frenchgate in afternoon sunlight shows off the different architectural styles of the houses.

Window boxes and
baskets full of flowers
provide colour throughout
the summer in the town.

Flower-fronted doorways (this picture shows
an escaping Jack Russell called Mattie).

Millgate House has its gardens open to the public;
this is showing the back view of the house and garden.

A snow covering – the view from Maison Dieu.

Oliver Duckett's Tower bathed in early morning winter sunshine.

One of the old narrow lanes leading to the Market Place.

Part of Millgate leading down to the waterfalls.

New steps leading down from
the Castle Walk to the river.

This house is used by RADS – Richmond Amateur Dramatic Society to practice their plays, which are performed in the Georgian Theatre Royal.

Part of the castle wall leading to the Barr. Note the
shadow of the castle keep on the gable end.

Faces in walls and gates.

Pretty cottage on a cobbled walkway behind the Market Place.

Wild foxgloves
growing in a driveway.

A great view of the Market Place from the top of the castle keep.

The bottom of the Market Place: the buildings arch round to the top.

Cyclists ready to enter the Richmond Meet race.

Richmond's answer to the Grand Prix.

They are off!

This page and opposite: The variety of shop fronts in the Market Place make it deeply attractive.

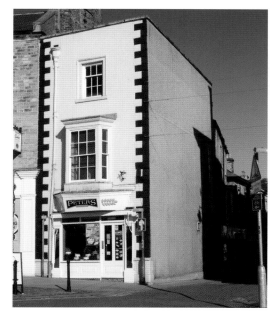

Three pictures illustrating
the town in Christmas guise –
the Market Cross, King Street
and Finkle Street.

An almost empty Market Place in early December.

Above:
The Friary Gardens – full of colourful flower beds
and benches to sit and admire the view.

Right:
The Friary Tower and War Memorial –
all within the Friary Gardens.

Newbiggin is a tree lined cobbled street leading towards the Market Place.
Newbiggin has its own little square.

The Richmond Operatic Society has its own meeting rooms, just off Newbiggin in a steep road called Bargate.

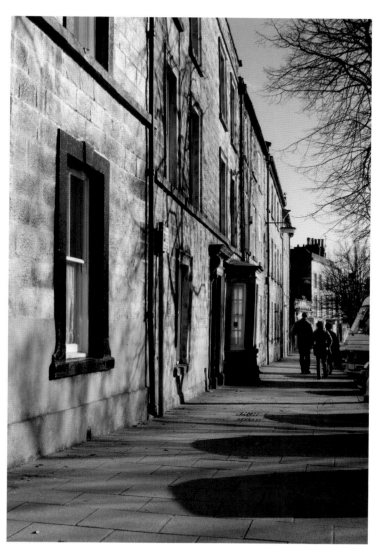

Looking down Newbiggin.

Autumn touching some of the trees in Newbiggin.

One of the Georgian-styled houses lining Newbiggin.

Above:
Bargate – this row of houses shows just how steep it is.

Right:
Double luck on a door frontage in Bargate.

Above:
Looking towards the bottom of Bargate.

Left:
Different door fronts.

55

Above:
Victoria Road takes you out towards the Dales:
this junction shows Westfields.

Right:
Richmond saw solar eclipse totality in 1927.

Houses with striking orange doors on the junction at Cravengate and Victoria Road.

Houses in Temple Square, a secluded part of Richmond off Cravengate.

**FRENCH MARKET
RICHMOND
Market Place
Sunday 19th
October**

Above:
French Market Sign – as Richmond
has a visit from them occasionally now.

Left:
Posters advertising forthcoming
plays at the Theatre Royal.

A sign pointing the way to the Market Place.

The door to the Garden Cottage, Richmond.

Looking up towards the Market Place in Millgate.

Top left:
A silver ball reflects the old
building across from it.

Top right:
Looking the other way in Millgate,
this road leads towards the
waterfalls and the Batts.

Left:
A shiny door handle
reflects Frenchgate.

The Station – now a thriving café, restaurant, cinema and place of interest.
It has also been a garden centre and was a great place for film & TV locations.

Looking back toward St Mary's church from Mercury Bridge (formerly Station Bridge).

Mercury Bridge from the castle keep.

The front of the Station.

Above:
The flower stall.

Left:
The Saturday Market – the stalls sell anything from pet food to fresh fruit and veg.

Stalls at the Farmers' Market that comes to Richmond every third Saturday of the month.

The French Market occasionally visits and is held on a Sunday.

Nicely displayed produce.

Above
Not forgetting the olives.

Left:
More French goodies to buy.

An interesting shop window inviting the visitor to come in and browse.

The sweet shop on the corner of Frenchgate.

The brightly coloured bistro in the middle of the Frenchgate channel.

The falls from the Batts – the brown coloured water is
due to the peat that is washed down in the River Swale.

Maison Dieu – one of the main roads leading in and out of Richmond.

Easby Abbey ruins – now looked after by English Heritage. The Abbey was founded in 1152.

Top end of Newbiggin showing the small cobbled square.

Holly Hill is situated on the other side of the River Swale; the road leads out towards the Garrison and Wensleydale.

The Georgian Theatre Royal – it shows the old theatre plus the new extension.
The theatre was built in 1788. Inside the theatre has been restored in true Georgian style.

Richmondshire Museum. The Victorian fountain outside in the garden used to be in the Market Place.
The museum also houses the TV series "All Creatures Great & Small" surgery set.

Trinity church situated in the centre of the Market Place. This is
home to the Green Howard Regimental Museum and Headquarters.

The Obelisk or Market Cross
from Castle Hill.

Green Bridge spanning the River Swale.

The start (or end) of Castle Walk.

The castle grounds host many an event – this one is showing off vintage Bentley cars.

Patrick Brompton lies beyond the rape field.

Part of the Coast to Coast Walk goes through Richmond, and in late spring the fields display a fantastic range of wild flowers.

A view of the Richmond skyline from the fields on the other side of the River Swale.

The chimneys of Richmond keep the chimney sweep, Mick Rochford, busy.
Here he is dealing with a chimney that was very blocked – hence no sign of a brush!

The Green at Catterick Village on a late summer's evening.

Brompton-on-Swale – a small village three miles from Richmond.

The hamlet Bolton on Swale, on the back road to Northallerton, the county town.

Kirby Hill is dominated by the church; here it is just before a winter snow storm.

Ravensworth Castle ruins are privately owned and sit just outside the village. Andreas Byrne

Ravensworth Village Green and houses.

Leyburn Market Place doubles as a car park on this cold winter's morning.

Large, long fields on the way to Redmire.

A prominent tree on MoD land lends itself as a silhouette against a perfect sunset.

The same tree against the backdrop of a stormy sky.

Gunnerside Flats: the valley floor here in Swaledale has a pattern of barns and stone walls.

Which way? Sign post outside Reeth guiding walkers across the fields.

A winter view from Keld, looking back towards Muker in Swaledale.

Winter scenes – the road across MoD land looking towards Leyburn.

Beyond Hawes, walkers braving the cold.

A very frosty morning near Middleham.

A tree at the old racecourse in Richmond, winter time.

Woodlands near Hartforth, Richmond, late spring.

A tree near Hartforth, Richmond, spring time.

Tree reflected in the River Ure, near Middleham.

An isolated barn at the top of Swaledale.

Crackpot Falls just outside the village of Low Row, Swaledale. Andreas Byrne

Looking down the Swaledale valley in mid August.

Clover and buttercups in a spring meadow near Muker, Swaledale.

Angram at the top of Swaledale – a barn with red doors, a magnet for photographers!

Reflections at Wainwath Falls, near Keld, Swaledale.

Above:
Riverside grasses catching the last rays of sun.

Left:
Dawn skies over Semer Water, near Hawes, Wensleydale. Andreas Byrne

Left:
A Richmondshire Sunset.

Right:
The upper falls at West Burton
on a late summer's evening.

Swaledale is famous for its flower meadows in
late spring. This is a stone barn near Crackpot.

Moulton Manor situated in a small village between Scorton and Middleton Tyas.

Moulton Village Green.

Moulton has a Wesleyan Church.

This is St Andrew's church, Moulton.

Moulton has the famous
Black Bull restaurant – hence the sign.

Busy junction –
Middleton Tyas.

An attic window.

An amusing sign in Catterick Village.

An interesting entrance – Catterick Village.

Two doors, one house in
Brompton-on-Swale.

A row of white houses – Melsonby.

The church – Melsonby.

Spring flowers on the
Green – Melsonby.

A broad view of Scorton from the Green. The Green is unusual in
that the road skirts round, making the Green like a big roundabout.

The old Grammar School in Scorton, now converted to residential use.

A drink of tea before hitting the road?

A pretty cottage on the Green.

The end houses in Gilling West.

Gilling West High Street runs the entire length of the village.

This page and opposite: Cameo shots of Gilling West.

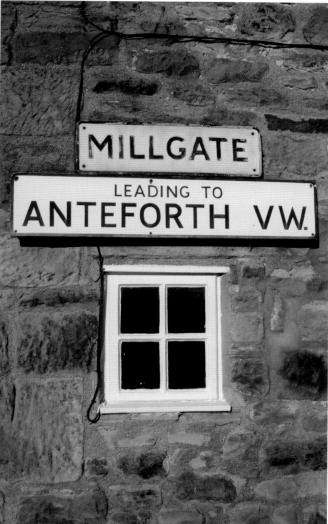

Best kept village trophy.

Functional Blacksmith's.

Above:
A pretty cottage front.

Right:
A hay field stretching from Skeeby towards the A1.

Skeeby Village.

A shallow stream runs in front of these houses in Aldbrough St John.

Above:
Part of the very large green at Aldbrough St John.

Right:
Reeth – a Mecca for walkers!

St Andrew's church,
Grinton, just before Reeth.

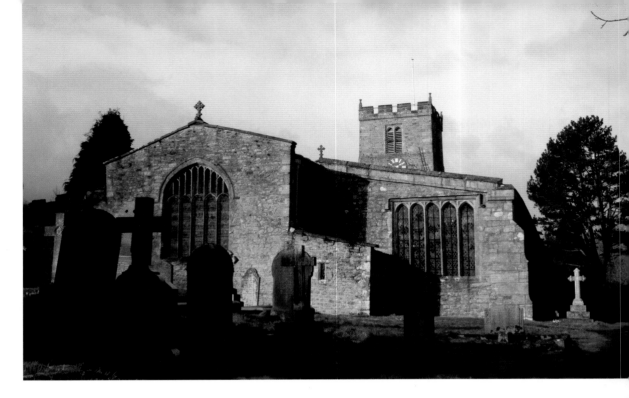

The Bridge Inn at Grinton.

The sheep on top of the Bridge Inn at Grinton!

Richmond town sign.